Liz Ashworth has been involved with and written about food for most for her life. She is passionate about preserving the Scottish food heritage and promotes her country's rich larder whenever she can. Author of *Teach the Bairns* series of traditional Scottish cookery books, she has written about her life experiences with food in the book *Orkney Spirit* and in many newspaper and magazine features and is a member of the Guild of Food Writers. She helps companies develop new products, particularly in the field of healthy eating, for which she has won various awards. She can be seen cooking in her own kitchen on YouTube and on her website www.lizashworth.co.uk.

'The potato is the most valuable gift the new world ever gave to the old.'

Dr Cramond, Cullen in
The Elgin Courant, 1899

The
William Shearer
Tattie Bible

Liz Ashworth

Illustrated by Bob Dewar

BIRLINN

First published in 2017 by
Birlinn Limited
West Newington House
10 Newington Road
Edinburgh
EH9 1QS

www.birlinn.co.uk

ISBN: 978 1 78027 469 0

British Library Cataloguing-in-Publication Data
A catalogue record for this book is available
from the British Library

Designed and typeset by Mark Blackadder

Printed and bound by Bell & Bain Ltd, Glasgow

Contents

Brunch

SHARPES EXPRESS   BIKINI   INFINITY   MARIS PIPER

The William Shearer Story

For five generations Shearer's have sourced seed potatoes. The annual William Shearer seed potato catalogue features over 40 aptly described seed potatoes, including heritage tattie favourites as well as more recent varieties.

The catalogue is researched and compiled by Richard, the fourth generation in the family business, which was established in 1857 by 21-year-old William Shearer. It is one of the few Orcadian firms with a pedigree dating back to the nineteenth century and is currently run by Richard, in partnership with his wife Audrey and sons William and Raymond.

Each year they source the best new varieties to recommend to tattie growers and select new names from the annual crop.

At William Shearer's you can not only buy seed tatties but the wherewithal to grow and harvest your own, and the equipment and ingredients with which to cook them too. A large wooden dresser displays tattie types old and new to pick and mix for a trial taste boil-up. All that is missing are recipes – but no longer.

This peedie (Orcadian for 'little') book, *The William Shearer Tattie Bible*, has been compiled to complete your enjoyment of a good tattie.

'William Shearer's is all my dream shops rolled into one! Fabulous local produce, amazing ironmongery and glorious garden department. I am seldom excited about shopping, but Shearer's is an Aladdin's cave of delicious and practical essentials.'

– Food writer Rosemary Moon, Jan. 2017

'We hope that on your visit to William Shearer you find what you are looking for and that you experience something of what a traditional family run business is all about – dedication to you, the customer.'

– Richard Shearer

http://www.williamshearer.co.uk

Introduction

'Lord look o'er us, three tatties among four of us.
Thank God, there's nae mair o'us.'
                From *We'll Say the Blessing*, Catriona Monro

In 1954 our family moved to a new house on the outskirts
of Elgin. Creating a garden was hard work. At a weekly
rate of three 'pennies', my sister and I helped remove endless
stones and grass roots. Dung arrived. Dusty Miller the
gardener came and planted 'tatties to clean the soil'.

We waited. Patience brought her reward – how good
were those tatties! That first pot of freshly boiled Duke of
York tatties, their floury interior bursting, nutty flavoured,
through golden skin, began a lifelong affinity. I love all
tatties, some more than others: Sharpe's Express, Keppleston
Kidneys, Pink Fir Apple, Golden Wonders, even the new
Bikini!

And the Westray Tattie! On a trip to the island, I was
dared to eat a steaming bowlful and duly obliged. At the
ferry the following day, the farmer arrived to deposit a large
bag of said tatties in the boot. Oh those tatties!

In 1868 Orcadian store-owner Thomas Warren sold Westray tatties for two shillings a barrel. He was my great-great-grandfather.

The potato was brought to Europe from Peru by the Spanish during the sixteenth century. There was in some countries, including Scotland, initial prejudice against the crop. Eventually around 1690 potatoes began to be grown in a few Scottish gardens but not in the open field until 1739, when 'persons travelled long distances to examine the new crop' (*The Elgin Courant*, 1899).

There was much to commend the potato. It helped eliminate chronic debilitating scurvy. Safely grown underground, less labour-intensive and providing a higher yield per acre, the potato provided a welcome alternative to grain crops, which often failed due to poor weather.

In 1783 the Icelandic volcano Laki erupted and a cloud of poisonous gas spread over Europe. Barley and oats withered and died in the field. At Lochlie Farm in Ayrshire, Robert Burns and his family had a hard time: 'The summer of 1783 was brutal' (*A Biography of Robert Burns* by James Mackay).

Kirk sessions, as guardians of the poor, were interested in the culture of potato. In 1783, with famine persisting, the session of Grange bought and distributed ten guineas' worth of turnip and potato seed, considering the importance of such crops in 'present scarcity'. Reluctance to grow the crop gradually dispelled and the tattie became an important dietary staple, often referred to as 'meat'.

In 1845 potato disease hit Ireland and the Icelandic volcano Hekla became active. When the disease affected Orkney some thought volcanic ash the cause. A writer describes 'dust so thick on the heather as to dim the bloom'. However, 'potatoes have never had such fine flavour, even in a good season since the disease began.'

The potato's ability to grow in poor soil and weather in the Highlands and Islands caused almost total dependence on it for food. This led to famine in 1846, when blight destroyed the crop and did so for several years. Many chose emigration to Canada or Australia, some assisted by the 'Laird'. A stark contrast to the violent evictions of the Clearances.

Agricultural practice improved and, with research, the emergence of disease-resistant varieties. In 1882 Colorado beetle devastated the American crop and Scottish seed potatoes were imported, up to 40,000 tons annually, mainly from Dundee. The boom lasted for 30 years from 1882 till 1912.

The Victorians embraced the potato, serving elaborate dishes. Shooting lunches often called for two hundred-weight of baked potatoes carried to the moors packed in sacks and skewered together to trap heat.

Potato rationing was not necessary during the Second World War due to a good home-grown supply, and the 'Potato Pete' campaign encouraged people to eat more because of their nutritional value.

The role of children in harvesting was important, hence the school October 'tattie' holidays. Children worked in the fields with their families lifting (howking) the tatties following a device aptly named a 'digger'. Many enduring friendships were made between families working in the tattie fields.

Today mechanisation has taken the effort out of the potato harvest and the 'tattie' holidays are simply 'time off school'. I am old enough to have gone 'tattie howking' – great fun but hard on the back and hands!

Home-grown tatties have sustained generations and the Scottish housewife must be congratulated on her creative skills.

It is amazing what you can make, bake or brew with a humble tattie.

This book is filled with information, tips and recipes to

enhance your tattie experience. There is guidance on how to cook tatties from plain boiled to the ultimate chip. There are classics like rumbledethumps, stovies and the Orkney pattie. Recipes from further afield include patatas bravas and bohnengemüse, a family recipe never before recorded – and new ones, specially created for this book.

A buried treasure indeed!

The recipes are graded according to their tattie rating (ease of making) and type of potato.

Tattie rating

 – simple

 – intermediate

 – more difficult

Type of potato

W   – Waxy
F   – floury
AR – all-rounder
N   – new

About tatties

'*Money* is the root of all evil, and yet it is such a useful root that we cannot get on without it any more than we can without potatoes.'

– Louisa May Alcott,
novelist (1832–88)

Tattie

The Scots call the potato a 'tattie'. Spelling and pronunciation vary – tatty, tatteh, tatie, taati, tatae, tatte, tautie, tawtie, tatoe, tattoo, tatta, tottie are a few.

Potatoes are good for you

An excellent source of plant protein, vitamins C and B6, they are free of fat, sodium and cholesterol. At around 110 calories per 100 grams (31 calories per ounce), potatoes are only fattening when cooked in fat/oil or eaten in large quantities. Naturally gluten-free, they contain iron, manganese, magnesium, phosphorus, copper, and more potassium than a banana. They are a good source of carbohydrate and fibre.

The healthiest way to eat potato is with the skin left on,

limiting nutrient loss in cooking, be it boiled, steamed or baked.

Tattie types

- Dry mealy potatoes with a high starch content cook to a dry, floury, fluffy texture.
- All round multipurpose potatoes with a medium starch content are used for most cooking methods.
- Waxy, moist potatoes containing less starch and more sugar are 'stickier' and firm when cooked.

Which type of tattie? Drop it in brine made of one part salt to eleven parts water. Waxy potatoes float, dry potatoes sink.

Heritage

Renewed interest in heritage varieties has seen the return of potatoes first grown over a century ago – for example:

Duke of York (1891) – mealy texture, full flavour and golden flesh.

Sharpe's Express (1901) – recognised by its pear shape and white fluffy flesh.

Pink Fir Apple (1850) – pink-skinned tubers of yellow waxy flesh.

Kerr's Pinks (1917) – floury, soft with excellent flavour. Originally grown in 1907 by J. Henry, Cornhill, Banff.

Golden Wonder (1904) – pale cream floury flesh. Boils rapidly, makes great chips!

Shetland Black – said to have come from a 1588 Spanish Armada shipwreck. Dark purple skins, intensely dry flesh and native to Shetland.

Red Emmalie, Highland Burgundy, and others too many to mention, all distinctive in appearance, flavour and cookability.

For more information, see *www.thompson-morgan.com/potato-selector-guide*, or William Shearer's Seed Potato Catalogue at *www.williamshearer.co.uk*.

Scottish seed potatoes are exported all over the world.

Grow your own
Growing potatoes in planters or grow bags is the perfect solution if you want to grow your own but have limited space. There's nothing like freshly dug home-grown tatties – even for Christmas!

See *www.thompson-morgan.com/how-to-grow-potatoes-in-bags* for step-by-step instructions.

Buying
Buy locally, in season.

Storing
Treat with care; potatoes bruise easily. Remove from polythene bags to avoid sweating. Keep in a cool, well aired, dark place. Exposure to light produces green skin containing a toxin: do not eat.

Cooking tips

- Add peeled raw potato to over-salted mince, soups or stews to absorb excess salt. Remove before serving.
- Thicken soups, stews and casseroles with mash.
- Save cooking water for soups and gravies.
- Drop peeled potatoes into lightly salted water to retain colour.

Bakers' tips

Pastry – potato pastry handles well, bakes evenly and retains crispness.

Victoria sponge – a spoon of mash beaten in with the eggs prevents curdling.

Rich cakes – add a spoon of mash while creaming fat and sugar. The cake will bake more evenly, cut without crumbling and stay moist longer.

Oatcakes – added mash makes an easy roll-and-cut dough, which bakes evenly crisp.

RECORD

SETANTA

KERR'S PINK

SARPO

Gluten-free
Potato flour – a creamy flour ground from the whole potato. It readily absorbs liquid. Use sparingly in breads, cakes and scones.

Potato starch – this is an allergen-free white powder which does not stand up to prolonged heat so is best used to thicken sauces toward the end of cooking. Use a balloon whisk. Added to baked goods it gives lightness. Use sparingly.

Other uses in the home
- Rub scalds with a slice of raw potato.
- Clean potato peel soothes swollen eyes.
- Potato water helps clean silver.
- Raw potato and bicarbonate of soda can remove stains and rust.
- Dry potato peel thrown on a fire saves coal.
- Potato juice makes good invisible ink.

Why are potatoes called spuds?
A false origin is that it came from the nineteenth-century group called *Society for the Prevention of an Unwhole-some Diet* – SPUD – who were against eating several foods including potatoes.

It may come from an old English name for the sharp narrow digging spade which is called a spud. Or possibly from the Dutch *spyd*, Norse *spjot* or Latin *spad*, meaning sword or dagger. The exact derivation is unknown.

How to cook a tattie

Boil

'The Scottish housewife at least knows how to boil a potato. Curiously, a perfectly boiled potato is a thing that is rarely to be had in the most expensive hotels and restaurants. They simply will not steam them dry.'
                    – F. Marian McNeill, *The Scots Kitchen*

Tips
Potato skin prevents the flesh being waterlogged in boiling, thereby retaining nutritional value, flavour and texture.

Cooked unpeeled potatoes keep longer in the fridge.

Peel potatoes thinly: most food value is directly under the skin.

Boil slowly to cook potatoes through evenly.

Potatoes of similar size will be cooked at the same time.

If boiled potatoes discolour, add a little lemon juice or vinegar to the cooking water.

Steam foil-wrapped fish or chicken and vegetables over potatoes for economy.

New potatoes
Scrub or scrape the delicate skin.

Cook in gently boiling salted water for 15–20 minutes till tender. Drain, steam and serve at once with butter and freshly chopped parsley.

Oatmealie tatties
Toss freshly boiled potatoes in butter, shake in a handful of toasted oatmeal, scatter with fresh parsley. A family favourite.

Crushed new tatties
Roughly crush with butter or olive oil, add herbs or spices. Serve hot.

Maincrop potatoes
Cover with cold water, add sea salt and boil, then reduce the heat to simmer to cook evenly. Potatoes are cooked when the point of a knife or skewer slides through. Drain through a colander or sieve, and shake. If possible take the pan and lid to open (cold) air, lift lid up and down a few times to create steam and dry the potatoes without losing heat. Cover with a dry tea towel or kitchen paper to absorb steam.

Benny's tattie tip
Neighbour Aubrey puts his pan of drained tatties on the doorstep to fluff – a tip learned on the family farm in County Armagh from his father Benny. It works. Cold air opens starch cells on the surface.

Steam
Thinly peeled or still in their jackets, old and new potatoes.

Steam over simmering salted water, 15 to 20 minutes for new potatoes and up to 30 minutes for maincrop, depending on size and variety.

Mash (Champit tatties)

Sheer indulgence – the ultimate comfort food.

Use floury or all-round maincrop like Maris Piper or King Edward. Boil potatoes of similar size, unpeeled or peeled thinly. Cover in cold salted water. Boil and simmer slowly till the point of a skewer goes smoothly through the flesh. Drain through a colander or sieve, shake, steam covered with a clean towel. Peel if needed. Mash or pass through a potato ricer or sieve.

For 450g (1lb) potatoes beat in 2 tablespoons of warm milk and 30g (1oz) of soft butter till smooth and fluffy. (Over-beating produces a gluey texture.) Taste, season and serve.

Mash can be stiff or soft depending on the potatoes and preferred taste. Potato puree is made by blitzing with added cream and/or melted butter to a sauce-like consistency.

Jazz up mash
Try the following: smoked cheese and chive; garlic and black pepper; grated lemon rind and olive oil; cooked mashed celeriac or parsnip.

Be adventurous, keep note of successes.

My top favourites are avocado or smooth stewed apple.

Dietary challenged mash
Beat with dairy-free milk or some of the cooking water. Add olive oil for a creamy finish.

Bake

A baked potato has a fluffy interior and a crisp skin.
Serve with or without a filling of which there are many.

The basics
Allow 1x 225g (8oz) potato per person (F/AR).
Scrub clean. Prick skin. Rub with oil and salt.

Baking options
Oven bake
Heat the oven to 200°C (fan 180°C), 400°F, Gas 6. Bake
    on the oven shelf or a tray for 1½ hours.
For speedier spuds parboil for 15 minutes, then drain,
    prick the skin, oil, salt, and bake for 40 to 45 minutes.
Half the potato lengthwise, lay flat on an oiled tray, bake
    for 25 to 35 minutes.
Microwave the prepared potato for 5 minutes, then oven
    bake for 45 minutes.

Slow cooker
On high power for 4½ hours, on low for 7½ hours.

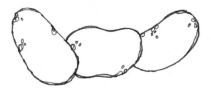

Microwave

Run under the cold tap, wrap each potato in kitchen paper, then cook on high for 3 or 4 minutes, turn and repeat. If a fork goes in easily, but the core is still a little firm, the potato is ready. Best to undercook, as an overcooked potato may burn or explode! Rest for 5 minutes for the heat to cook the centre and fluff the inside.

Barbecue

Foil wrap. Bake for 1 to 2 hours. Parboil to cut time.

To serve, up end, cut a cross on top, push in the sides and ends gently to fluff open, ready for butter!

A few ideas

Simply fill

Split and add cheese, coleslaw, baked beans, tuna mayo, grated cheese with chopped bacon.

Loaded potato skins

Split, scoop out, leaving 5mm (¼in.) rim. Mash flesh with cheese and bacon. Pile in skins, oven bake or grill crisp. Serve hot, topped with sour cream and chopped chives.

Crispy potato skins

Brush scooped skins with oil, grill or oven bake to crisp. Serve with a choice of dips or fillings.

Roast

Varieties like Maris Piper, King Edward, Golden Wonder, potatoes with a high starch content, make crisp roasters. Check new varieties on: *www.thompson-morgan.com/potato-selector-guide*.

Serves 4

600g (1lb 5oz) potatoes, thinly peeled and cut to even size (F/AR/N)
Sea salt
2 tablespoons oil or fat

Suitable roasting temperature from 180°C (fan 160°C), 350°F, Gas 4 to 200°C (fan 180°C) 400°F, Gas 6, allows an organised cook to fill the oven.

Cover the potatoes with cold salted water, boil for 8 to 10 minutes. Drain through a colander or sieve, and shake well to fluff. If liked, score with the prongs of a fork, creating important cracks which roast crisp.

Suitable fats and oils

Oils – rapeseed, sunflower, grapeseed, corn, olive, flavoured oils.

Fats – duck, goose, lard, dripping, or suet and salt.

Heat the 2/3 tbsp oil/fat in a heavy baking tray or roasting tin. Shake the potatoes into the hot oil/fat and turn to coat. Roast till golden, turning occasionally. Drain on kitchen paper in a heated dish and serve. Keep crisp in a warm oven for 15 minutes.

Skinny roasters

Brush parboiled potatoes with oil. Roast on a non-stick tray, turning occasionally.

New potatoes

No need to parboil. Roast small even-sized potatoes in their jackets. Turn frequently.

The ultimate chip

I worked weekends in the Larder at Rothiemurchus while my son Alan and his friend James helped at the fish farm nearby. On our homeward journey we began our quest for the ultimate chip. Armed with a list of venues, we ticked off another each week. From soggy, half-cold to golden crisp we tried them all – some more than once!

A good chip is a joy to eat. It should have a fluffy centre with outside crunch, crisp to the last chip.

The basics
Use floury or medium floury potatoes – Maris Piper, King Edward, Golden Wonder. Waxy potatoes make soggy chips. Thick chips are less fattening than thin or crinkle. Parcooked chips can be kept for up to one day in the fridge.

Serves 2 to 3
600g (1lb 5oz) potatoes, washed
2 litres (3½pt) groundnut, sunflower or corn oil
Sea salt

Peel on or peeled, cut thick or thin chips.
Rinse in cold water, drain, and dry on a clean tea towel.

Frying method

Use a large pan and chip basket or free-standing fryer.
Only fill the pan one third – oil rises as it cooks. Be safe.
Have a fire blanket or extinguisher near.

Heat the oil in the fryer to 130°C or till a raw chip
begins to float and fry. Cook small batches.

Half-fill the chip basket, lower into the oil and fry
slowly till the chips are tender but not browned. Drain
on kitchen paper. Heat the oil to 180°C or till a chip
turns golden and crisp. Lower in the chips to fry till crisp
and golden. Drain on kitchen paper, serve at once
sprinkled with sea salt.

Parboil method

Cover the chips in cold salted water, boil, then simmer
for 5 minutes. Drain, shake dry and cool on a wire rack.
Heat the oil to 140°C. Fry the chips till just colouring.
Drain on kitchen paper. Heat the oil to 180°C, fry till
golden. I found chips made by this method stay crisp
longer.

Oven chips

Cut thick chips, soak for 10 minutes in cold water, drain
and dry. Heat the oven to 200°C (fan 180°C) 400°F, Gas
6. Oil a heavy baking tray, heat for 3 minutes. Put the
chips in one layer on the tray and brush with oil. Bake
for 20 minutes, turning once or twice. Drain on kitchen
paper and serve.

Sauté potato (Fried tatties)

Sauté means to cook quickly, from the French *sauter*, to jump.

Allow 225g (8oz) sliced potatoes per person, cooked or raw (F/AR/N)
Butter or oil
Choose a thick-bottomed frying pan

Sauté raw potato
Cut peeled or unpeeled potatoes into 5mm (¼in.) slices, soak in cold water, drain and dry on kitchen paper. Fry at medium heat for 5 minutes on each side till golden and cooked through. Some potatoes take longer than others. Drain on kitchen paper and serve.

Sauté cooked potato
Cut cooked potato, with or without peel, into 5mm (¼in.) slices. Fry for 2 or 3 minutes on each side till crisp. Some potatoes colour faster than others. Drain on kitchen paper and serve.

New potatoes
Cut raw or cooked small new potatoes in half lengthwise before frying.

Potato gratin

If ever there was a kitchen game, set, and match, it is a potato gratin.

Gratin is defined as 'baked with encrusted browned surface'. The traditional heat-resistant dish is shallow and sloping sides mean a wider surface for the all-important crust.

Sliced, grated or shredded, potato absorbs flavour as it bakes.

A basic recipe for a simple gratin from the Canadian *Potatoes* booklet of 1958.

Serves 4

1 medium onion, peeled and thinly sliced
30g (1oz) butter
4 medium potatoes, peeled and thinly sliced, shredded
    or grated (F/AR/W/N)
Sea salt
Ground black pepper
120ml (4fl oz) water or stock
85g (3oz) grated cheese
30g (1oz) breadcrumbs
15g (½oz) butter if liked

Turn on the oven at 180°C (fan 160°C), 350°F, Gas 4. Sweat the onion in butter till soft. Butter a suitable dish. Starting and ending with potatoes, layer with the onions, seasoning each. Pour stock or water over the dish and bake covered for 25 to 30 minutes. Mix the cheese and breadcrumbs. Remove the dish cover, sprinkle with the cheese and crumbs. Turn the temperature to 200°C (fan 180°C), 400°F, Gas 4. Bake the gratin for 10 minutes to brown or crisp under a medium hot grill.

Try adding

Chopped ham or bacon

Smoked haddock and tomato

Sliced mushrooms

Chopped chicken or turkey

Replace water with stock, double cream, or a pouring white or cheese sauce

Get gratin-ing!!

Home-made tattie crisps

Once made in Orkney in several flavours, Pomona
Crisps had a certain home-made quality about them.
Bring them back!

Serves 4

2 medium-size potatoes, peeled and thinly sliced (F/AR) –
   use a mandolin if you have one
Oil or dripping to deep fry
Sea salt

Put the potato slices in a bowl under slow running cold
water for 30 minutes. Drain and dry thoroughly on
kitchen paper. Heat the oil to 180°C, 350°F or till a slice
of bread takes 1 minute to brown slowly in the oil.
Prepare a tray covered in kitchen paper. Deep fry in small
batches. Turn frequently with a slotted heat-resistant
spoon. It will take 2 or 3 minutes for the slices to
become golden. Drain on kitchen paper. Enjoy freshly
fried, sprinkled with sea salt. Store on kitchen paper in a
sealed container.

Microwave
Lay potato slices on a suitable oiled plate. Brush with oil.
Microwave on high power in 30 second bursts. Turn as
needed. Remarkable results – try it.

From one tattie many crisps grow.

Traditional tattie recipes

From Scotland

Clapshot

Traditionally served at Burns Suppers and Harvest Homes.

Serves 4
Takes 15 minutes to make

450g (1lb) potato, cooked in boiling salted water,
    drained and steamed dry (F/AR)
450g (1lb) turnip, cooked in boiling salted water and drained
60g (2oz) butter
Finely chopped chives or spring onion
Sea salt and ground black pepper

Melt the butter in a deep saucepan, add the potatoes and
turnip. Mash together, then beat smooth with a wooden
spoon. Season to taste with plenty of ground black
pepper and sea salt. (Some add a pinch of ground
ginger.) Stir in the chives. Serve hot. If the turnip is pale,
add a little carrot or sweet potato while cooking.

Clapshot pies
Cover mince, stew or haggis with clapshot. Sprinkle with
grated cheddar and oven bake at 180°C (fan 160°C),
350°F, Gas 4 for 25 minutes.

Burns Supper starter
Spoon haggis into buttered ramekin dishes, top with clapshot. Oven bake for 10 minutes. Serve hot.

Rumbledethumps

'Rumble' means mashed together and 'thump' to bash down. This traditional Borders dish is like Scottish bubble and squeak!

___

Serves 2
Takes 25 minutes to make

225g (8oz) cold cooked mashed potatoes (F/AR)
185g (6oz) cold cooked cabbage or sprouts – some recipes add turnip
30g (1oz) butter
1 small onion or a few spring onions, peeled and chopped
Sea salt and ground black pepper
60g (2oz) grated mature cheddar cheese

___

Melt the butter in a deep pan, add the onion and cook on low heat to soften. Add the potatoes and cabbage or sprouts, 'rumble and thump' together, season to taste. Turn into a buttered ovenproof dish, top with the grated cheese and brown under a pre-heated grill. Serve hot.

Add extra 'rumble'
Stir in: cooked meat, chicken, turkey, cooked bacon, smoked fish, or baked beans.

Colcannon

Traditional mash from the Highlands.

Serves 4
450g (1lb) mashed potatoes (F/AR)
450g (1lb) cold cooked carrot, turnip and cabbage, mashed together
60g (2oz) butter
2 teaspoon brown sauce
Sea salt and ground black pepper

Melt the butter in a pan, add the potatoes and vegetables.
Keep stirring over medium heat to mix till bubbling.
Season to taste with salt, pepper and brown sauce. Serve
hot.

Kailkenny

The name is thought to be a corruption of Colcannon.

Serves 2
225g (8oz) cold mashed potato (F/AR)
225g (8oz) cold cooked cabbage
3 tablespoons double cream
Sea salt and ground black pepper

Mix the potatoes and cabbage together, beat in the cream
and heat slowly, stirring continuously, over medium heat.
Season to taste and serve very hot.

Champ

Beat creamy mashed potatoes (F/AR) with plenty butter
and chopped spring onions and serve hot.

Sam's hairy tatties

Similar continental dishes are described as emulsions of salt fish, oil and potatoes. 'Hairy Tatties' says it all!

An Orkney take on the classic by chef Sam Britten.

Serves 4 as a starter

Step 1
150g (3½oz) salt fish soaked in cold water for 24 hours

Step 2
300ml (½pt) milk
½ shallot, peeled
1 bay leaf
500g (1lb 2oz) potatoes, peeled and cut into small pieces (F)
200g (7oz) butter
185g (6oz) white crab meat

To serve:
Home-pickled cucumber or small gherkins
Shallots, peeled and cut in thin rings
Fresh lemon juice
Parsley oil – see overleaf

Simmer the drained salt fish in milk with the shallot and bay leaf for 15 to 20 minutes. Remove the fish and flake. Strain and reserve the milk. Boil the potatoes in salted water till very tender. Drain, steam dry, then pass through a ricer or sieve. Beat the warm potatoes with butter (allow 50g (1¾oz) butter to 100g (3½oz) potato) to emulsify. Heat the finished mash by stirring over low heat, adding a drop of reserved milk to prevent it from splitting. Treat the finished mash like mayonnaise because of the high fat content. Beat in the flaked salt fish and crab meat (as much or as little as you like). Beat off the stove until you see fish fibres making it 'hairy'.

Serve a small amount in the centre of a bowl with home-pickled cucumbers, parsley oil and fresh shallot rings dressed in lemon juice.

Parsley oil
Blanch a handful of fresh parsley in boiling salted water for 10 seconds. Drain, then drop in iced water. Drain, blitz with olive oil to a smooth green puree. Store sealed in the fridge.

Hairy tatties with garlic and olive oil

Thank you to Catherine Brown for this recipe taken from her book *Scottish Seafood: Its History and Cooking*.

Serves 4

Step 1
500g (1lb 2oz) heavily salted fish, soaked 12 to 24 hours depending on saltiness

Step 2
300ml (10fl oz) extra virgin olive oil, warmed
4–6 cloves garlic
500g (1lb 2oz) potatoes, cooked and mashed (F)
50ml (4 tablespoons) hot milk
1 tablespoon chopped fresh parsley

Drain the fish, cover with cold water, boil, turn off the heat, cover and leave for 15 to 20 minutes. Cool, lift onto a plate, and remove bones. Put into a food processor, add garlic and a little warm oil, blend for a few seconds and repeat with the rest of the oil. Add the parsley and whiz till smooth. Pour into a bowl, beat in the mash and whisk in the hot milk till light and 'hairy'. Taste and season. Serve with warm toast and poached or boiled eggs.

Stovies

F. Marian McNeill (*The Scots Kitchen*, 1929) suggested 'to stove' has French origins. However Catherine Brown (*Scottish Cookery*, 1985) discovered there is a Scottish and North of England word 'stove'. It means a slow sweated, steamed stew cooked in a covered pot.

No matter, the recipe is not precise, more a satisfying versatile one-pot meal.

The basics

_____

Serves 4
1.1kg (2½lb) potatoes, peeled and thickly sliced (F/AR)
2 medium onions, peeled and sliced
45g (1½oz) fat – bacon, dripping, butter or oil
Water or stock
Sea salt and ground black pepper
Pinch of nutmeg or allspice

_____

Choose a strong deep pan with tight-fitting lid. Heat the fat, add the onion and potato. Stir together, cover and cook on low heat for up to 10 minutes. Stir frequently. Add a little water, stock or gravy. More liquid makes wetter stovies. Stir, cover, cook on low, stirring occasionally, till the potatoes start to disintegrate.

Add chopped cooked meat or fish. Season to taste with salt and plenty black pepper. Add nutmeg or allspice if liked.

Different tastes

Make browned pieces of potato to mix through by cooking to a crisp layer on the pan base then stir through.

Add a little liquid, and steam uncovered for dry stovies. Beat well, adding more gravy or sauce to taste to make a smooth, softer eat.

Stovies tried and tested

Roast beef – dripping, add roast gravy and chopped beef to taste.

Roast turkey – created and cooked over a campfire for cubs who queued for seconds begging to scrape the pan! Add chopped roast turkey or chicken and gravy. Leftover stuffing too, if liked.

Cullen skink – butter, onion, chopped smoked haddock, double cream and black pepper. Winner of the 'Exotic Stovie' prize, Huntly Hairst 2012.

Corned beef – beat in chopped corned beef, and brown sauce or gravy.

Try – black pudding, haggis, sausages, mince, stew, chickpeas, smoked salmon.

What will you add to the stovie pot?

Orkney pattie

What is an Orkney pattie? Every Orkney chipper has its secret family formula but, despite extensive 'in the chippie' research, its origins remain elusive.

Makes 10 patties
85g (3oz) leftover mince mixed with
1 small onion, peeled, chopped and lightly fried
450g (1lb) mashed potato (F/AR)
60g (2oz) fresh breadcrumbs
Sea salt and ground black pepper
Oil to deep fry

Batter
60g (2oz) self-raising flour
¼ teaspoon salt
Scant 200ml (7fl oz) cold water

Mix the mince, onion, potato and breadcrumbs together, season with salt and plenty of black pepper. Shape into patties (a thick round scone-shape), 60g (2oz) weight. Dust with flour and chill for at least 30 minutes. Sift the flour and salt into a bowl, whisk in the cold water to make a smooth batter, rest for 30 minutes. Heat the oil to 180°C or till a slice of bread turns golden in 1 minute. Flour the patties if sticky, dip into batter to coat and slide into hot oil. Fry for 5 minutes, turning to brown evenly. Drain on kitchen paper and serve hot with chips. Patties can be frozen before battering and cooked from frozen at 170°C for 6 to 8 minutes to ensure they are cooked through.

A joy of indulgence only fully appreciated eaten fresh from an Orkney chipper!

Mince 'n' tatties wi' a tattie doughball

Interviewed on Radio Scotland's *Kitchen Café*, accordionist Phil Cunningham admitted that a plate of 'mince 'n' tatties' is his taste of home.

Serves 4
450g (1lb) steak mince
1 medium onion, peeled and chopped
45g (1½oz) oatmeal
Sea salt
Ground black pepper
Boiling water

Cook the mince in a saucepan on medium heat, stirring with a wooden spoon to brown and separate the meat grains. Add the onion and stir to brown a little. Lower the heat, stir in the oatmeal with enough water to make a rich gravy. Simmer covered for 35 minutes. Stir occasionally to prevent sticking, adding water if needed, taste and season. Make doughballs.

Makes 4
85g (3oz) self-raising flour
1 level teaspoon baking powder
¼ teaspoon sea salt
30g (1oz) mashed potato (F/AR)
45g (1½oz) suet
Water

Sift the flour, baking powder and salt into a bowl. Add
the mashed potato and suet and fork together. Mix to a
soft elastic dough with cold water. Turn onto a floured
board, divide in four and shape each into a soft ball. Stir
the mince, adding more water if needed to ensure plenty
gravy. Gently drop into the simmering mince, cover to
trap steam, which will cook the dumplings. Leave for 12
to 15 minutes till firm and soaked in gravy.

Serve with mash – see page 24.

From further afield

Spudnuts – two ways

Across the pond a song was written about delivering 'spuds':

> *It's Bud the spud from the bright red mud*
> *Rollin' down the highway smilin'*
> *The spuds are big on the back of his rig*
> *And they're from Prince Edward Island.*

Named after Spudnut, once a chain of doughnut eateries.

Makes 7 doughnuts
115g (4oz) self-raising flour
1 teaspoon baking powder
60g (2oz) butter or margarine
60g (2oz) mashed potato (F/AR)
1 small teaspoon vanilla essence or 1 level teaspoon
    mixed spice or ground cinnamon
30g (1oz) caster sugar
1 small egg, beaten
Caster sugar to coat

To oven bake

Turn on the oven at 190°C (fan 170°C), 375°F, Gas 5. Oil a heavy baking tray. Sift the flour and baking powder into a bowl. Add the butter and mashed potato and fork together. Stir in the sugar. Mix to a soft light dough with the beaten egg. Heat the baking tray for a few minutes. Turn the dough onto a well-floured board, sprinkle with flour and flatten with the palm of your hand to 1cm (½in.) thickness. Cut with a round 6cm (2½in.) cutter. Rework scraps lightly. Lay on the hot tray. Bake for 10 to 12 minutes till risen and golden. Shake the caster sugar on a sheet of baking paper. Toss the hot spudnuts in sugar one at a time, pressing the sugar in gently. Cool on a wire tray. Enjoy warm and freshly baked.

To deep fry

Heat oil to 180°C, 350°F or when bread takes a minute to brown in the oil. Cook doughnuts for 3 minutes on each side till cooked through. Toss in caster sugar, cool on a wire tray and serve warm.

Spudnuts stay soft for 24 hours and can be frozen in a sealed container for 4 weeks.

Bombay potatoes

Over 30 years ago I joined a group of like-minded housewives to make, bake and sell. We called ourselves Polmont Crafts. One, Anne, grew up in India; this is her recipe.

Serves 4
375g (12oz) cooked potatoes cut into quarters (F/AR/W/N)
2 tablespoons cooking oil
½ teaspoon mustard seeds
½ teaspoon cumin seeds
¼ teaspoon turmeric
¼ teaspoon chilli flakes
¼ teaspoon sea salt
1 tablespoon hot water
Chopped fresh coriander to serve

Heat the oil in a pan on medium heat. Drop in a few mustard seeds – when they pop add the seeds and spices. Stir for 1 minute then add salt and potatoes. Stir fry for 4 minutes. Turn the heat to low, add water and cover the pan. Steam for 5 minutes. Serve hot scattered with chopped fresh coriander.

May be eaten in a sauce made with 115g (4oz) chopped tomato, clove of garlic and piece of root ginger blitzed with 1 teaspoon of garam masala.

Boxty in the pan

Boxty is a traditional Irish potato pancake. Its popularity inspired the rhyme:

> *Boxty on the girdle, and boxty in the pan,*
> *The wee one in the middle is for Mary Anne.*
> *Boxty on the girdle, and boxty in the pan,*
> *If you can't bake boxty sure you'll never get a man.*

Makes 8 pancakes
100g (3½oz) grated raw potato (F/AR)
100g (3½oz) mashed potato (F/AR)
115g (4oz) plain flour
½ teaspoon sea salt
10g (2 teaspoons) baking powder
2 eggs, beaten
75ml (2½fl oz) milk to mix
Oil or butter to fry

Put the grated potato into a clean cloth, twist and squeeze to remove moisture. Sift the flour, salt and baking powder into a bowl. Add the grated and mashed potato, eggs and enough milk to make a stiff batter. Heat a heavy frying pan on low to medium heat. Add a tablespoon of oil or butter. Do not overheat the pan. These thick pancakes must be cooked for 3 to 4 minutes on each side to avoid raw middles! A timer is handy. Drop tablespoons of batter into the pan and flatten a little with the back of the spoon. Cook for 3 minutes or till bubbles rise and burst on the surface. Turn to bake for 3 or 4 more minutes till cooked through. Drain on kitchen paper. Serve hot. Traditionally eaten spread with butter and a sprinkling of sugar, and at breakfast fried as part of the famous Ulster fry.

Modern recipes add spices, herbs and garlic.

Scandinavian potato casserole

A warm smooth light soufflé, which does not collapse!

Real comfort food that leaves you wishing there was more.

Makes a starter for 4 or light meal for 2

300g (10oz) cooked, riced or mashed potatoes (F/AR)
60ml (4 tablespoons) milk
Single cream to mix
¼ teaspoon sea salt
Ground black pepper
Pinch of nutmeg (optional)
30g (1oz) grated parmesan or similar hard cheese
2 eggs, separated

Turn on the oven at 180°C (fan 160°C), 350°F, Gas 4. Butter 4 x 10cm (4in.) ramekins. Beat the potatoes smooth with the milk and one tablespoon of cream. Beat in the seasoning, egg yolks and cheese to a smooth dropping consistency, adding more cream if needed. Beat the egg whites stiff and fold in. Pour into the ramekins. Bake in a water bath for 15 to 20 minutes till risen and golden. Serve hot as a starter. Alternatively, pour into a buttered 75ml (1¼pt) soufflé dish and bake for 25 to 30 minutes till risen and golden. Enjoy hot.

Patatas bravas

In 1933 Madrid, a small bar called Las Bravas served fried
potatoes with spicy tomato sauce, creating 'patatas bravas'.
The dish has gone international!

Serves 4 people
750g (1lb 10oz) potatoes, peeled and cut into bite-size
    pieces (F/AR/N)
Sea salt
15ml (1tbs) olive oil

Turn on the oven at 200°C (fan 180°C), 400°F, Gas 4.
Cook the potatoes in boiling salted water for 5 minutes.
Drain through a sieve or colander, shake dry. Heat a
heavy baking tray in the oven. Toss the dry potatoes with
olive oil and scatter in a single layer on the hot baking
tray. Roast for 15 to 20 minutes till brown and crisp,
turning once. Meanwhile make the sauce.

Tomato (brava) sauce
15ml (1 tablespoon) olive oil
1 medium onion, peeled and chopped
2 cloves garlic, peeled and crushed (optional)
½ teaspoon smoked paprika
Pinch of cayenne pepper
½ teaspoon balsamic or sherry vinegar
1 tin chopped tomatoes (225g/8oz)
Sea salt

Heat the olive oil in a pan on medium heat, sweat the onion and garlic till soft. Stir to prevent sticking. Add paprika, cayenne, vinegar and tomatoes. Simmer for 15 minutes. Taste and season. Serve chunky or blitz smooth.

Quick sauce
Stir paprika, cayenne, crushed garlic and sherry vinegar into tomato ketchup to taste.

Drain the potatoes on kitchen paper, toss into a heated bowl and sprinkle with sea salt. Serve sauce on the side. Provide eaters with small plates, a spoon and fork.

Mutti's bohnengemüse

I leave my friend Gisela to tell the story:

> My grandmother was born in Alsace-Lorraine. My grand-
> father was an engineer in the coalmines; he and his young
> family came to the Ruhr district around 1910. This recipe
> came with them and is only known and loved in my family.
> I don't know more about it. German bohnenkraut is
> important for flavour.

Mutti (Gisela's mother) made the best. I love it.

Serves 4

450g (1lb) floury potatoes, peeled and sliced thinly (F)
450g (1lb) onions, peeled and sliced
450g (1lb) tomatoes, skinned and sliced
450g (1lb) whole fresh young green beans, topped and tailed
450g (lb) lean pork, trimmed and cut into slices
Sea salt
Ground black pepper
Handful of summer savory (bohnenkraut), thyme or oregano
150ml (¼pt) vegetable stock or water

Use a deep heavy pan or casserole. Layer the vegetables on
top of the pork, adding herbs, seasoning as you go. Pour in
the stock or water. Cover tightly. Cook slowly for at least 2
hours on very low heat on the cooker. Check occasionally,
add more liquid if needed but do not stir. Alternatively,
oven cook at 140°C (fan 120°C), 275°F, Gas 1.

Slow cooking is important. Serve hot in warm bowls
with crusty bread and a glass of pils.

Brunch

Tattie scones

Each June, at Piping Hot Forres, the World Tattie Scone
Competition (inspired by the late David Urquhart)
invites lovers of this delicacy to be creative.

My neighbour, Rev. Bill Miller, was partial to a tattie
scone, warm from my kitchen – a simple recipe with
potential!

Makes 8 scones

225g (8oz) plain boiled potatoes mashed smooth or pressed
    through a ricer (F/AR)
Approximately 60g (2oz) self-raising flour
15g (½oz) melted butter
¼ teaspoon sea salt
Milk if needed to mix

Heat a heavy frying pan or girdle on medium. Put the
potatoes, butter, flour and salt into a bowl. Stir together,
adding milk if needed to make a light smooth dough. Turn
onto a floured board and knead gently. Half, and work into
two balls. Roll each to a thin circle on a floured board. Cut
both into four triangles. Test the girdle heat with a sprinkle
of flour. If it's too hot it will burn; golden brown shows the
pan is ready. Bake the scones for 3 minutes on each side.
Keep warm in a clean tea towel on a wire tray. Enjoy
warm. Equally good fried as part of a traditional breakfast.

Riced potatoes make lighter scones.

Grate tattie oat pancakes

My cooking friend Moira and I concoct recipes to demonstrate in the food fayre at the annual Nairn Show. This one was a hit.

Serves 4
225g (8oz) cooked potato, roughly grated (F/AR/W)
1 small carrot, peeled and finely grated
1 tablespoon porridge oats
1 teaspoon grated lemon rind
1 egg
Sea salt
Ground black pepper
Butter or oil to cook

To serve:
4 fresh eggs at room temperature
4 slices black pudding
Freshly chopped parsley

In a bowl mix the grated potato and carrot and the oats, season with sea salt and ground black pepper and grated lemon rind. Mix with the beaten egg. Boil a pan of salted water and reduce the heat to below simmer. Heat a tablespoon of butter or oil in a large frying pan on medium heat. Drop 4 tablespoons of potato mixture into the pan, pressing with the back of the spoon to make a flat pancake. Cook for 3 minutes on each side. Drain on kitchen paper. Keep warm while frying the black pudding till crisp on each side. To poach the eggs, break each into a teacup and slide into the hot water for 3 to 4 minutes. Do not boil. Serve each pancake on a warm plate, topped with black pudding and a softly poached egg. Garnish with chopped parsley.

Nairn Show

Hash bean browns

At our annual Guide camp we took turns to cook. A memorable concoction involved frying tatties and baked beans over the fire. This version omits smoke flavour and twigs!

Serves 4
500g (1lb 2oz) chunks of cooked potato, roughly crushed (F/AR)
45g (1½oz) butter, smoked bacon fat or oil
½ onion, peeled and finely chopped
Sea salt and ground black pepper
1 small tin of baked beans, drained

Heat a heavy frying pan at medium. Melt half the fat, stir in the onion to soften, add the potatoes, season and stir together. Add the drained beans and stir in. Press together to make a pancake, and cook for 10 minutes or till the underside forms a thick browned crust. Take a flat plate large enough to cover the pan, loosen the potato pancake, then invert the pan to deposit the pancake on the plate, browned side up. Melt the rest of the fat, and slip the pancake back in the pan for another 8 to 10 minutes to brown. Cut into quarters and serve hot.

Store in the fridge for up to 3 days.

Bacon floddies

As a result of famine in the mid 1800s, total dependency on potato as a food crop waned. The excess fed pigs instead – perhaps inspiration for this rhyme:

Holy Brethren, is it not a sin? To put tattie peelings into the bin. The peel feeds pigs – The pigs feed you – Now Holy Brethren, is that not true?

Serves 2
225g (8oz) potato, peeled and grated (F/AR/N)
1 small onion or a few spring onions, peeled and chopped
85g (3oz) smoked bacon, chopped
30g (1oz) self-raising flour
1 large egg, beaten
Sea salt and ground black pepper
Oil or bacon fat to fry
Grated cheese

Put the grated potato into a clean tea towel, twist to squeeze out excess liquid. Shake the potato into a bowl, season, mix in the chopped onion, bacon and flour. Stir in the egg. Heat the oil or fat in a frying pan at medium heat. Drop tablespoons of mix into the pan to cook for 3 or 4 minutes on each side till golden. Slow fry to ensure each floddie is cooked through. Drain on kitchen paper. Serve hot topped with grated cheese.

Granny Mac's fish cakes

Mrs Kate Maclaren (Granny Mac) was pre-war Principal
of the Girls' Technical School in Elgin. Her son
Donald and my father were close friends, and when
Donald emigrated to Canada, Granny Mac became part
of our family. A signed copy of her cookery book
published in 1938 has been handed down. This is her
recipe.

Makes 4 x 85g (3oz) fish cakes
225g (8oz) mashed potato (F/AR)
115g (4oz) flaked flesh of an Arbroath Smokie
10g (¼oz) melted butter – add more to drier mash
Sea salt and ground black pepper
Plain flour
Beaten egg to coat
Breadcrumbs to coat
Butter or oil to cook

Put the mash into a bowl, fork together with the flaked
fish and melted butter, taste and season. Divide into five
equal portions. Shape into round flat cakes on a floured
board. Chill for 10 minutes. Make a production line. Pour
beaten egg on a plate, next breadcrumbs on a sheet of
baking paper, lastly a clean plate. Dip each fish cake into
egg, drain, lay in the crumbs, use paper to lift and coat,
press the crumbs lightly into the surface, lift onto the

plate. Shallow fry in melted butter, oil or a mixture, at medium heat for 4 minutes on each side till golden. Drain on kitchen paper and serve with lemon mayonnaise.

Lemon mayonnaise
Sister Sue's recipe, Granny Mac would approve!

Beat grated lemon rind and juice into mayonnaise to taste. Season and serve.

Sausage, bacon and apple rolls

A spur-of-the-moment recipe.

Makes 18 cocktail-size rolls

Pastry:
115g (4oz) self-raising flour
45g (1½oz) mashed potato (F/AR)
60g (2oz) margarine
Pinch of sea salt

Filling:
100g (3½oz) pork sausage meat
75g (2½oz) smoked bacon, finely chopped
30g (1oz) tangy eating apple, finely grated
Ground black pepper
Beaten egg, to glaze

Turn on the oven at 180°C (fan 160°C), 350°F, Gas 4.
Use a food processor or mixer to blend pastry ingredients
into a clean dough. Alternatively, rub the margarine into
the flour, stir in the potato and knead together. Leave to
rest. Mix the filling ingredients together. Shape into two
sausage-like lengths on a floured board. Lay on a plate.
Cut pastry in half. Roll each piece to a rectangle approximately 30cm x 15cm (12in. x 6in.). Brush with beaten
egg. Lay the sausage 1cm (½in.) from the long edge of

each. Lift the pastry over the sausage and roll into a
cylinder across the strip to seal, ending with the join
underneath. Divide each roll into 9 and lay on a baking
tray. Cut a slit on top of each, brush with beaten egg.
Bake for 15 to 20 minutes till crisp. Enjoy hot or cold.

Mix a teaspoon of chutney or pesto in the filling
instead of apple.

Tattie omelette

My late father was a dab hand at whisking up a mean omelette. Spanish tortilla and Italian frittata are, in my humble opinion, not a patch on Dad's.

Serves 2

225g (8oz) cooked potato, cut into bite-sized pieces (F/AR/W/N)
15g (½oz) butter
4 large eggs, beaten with 2 tablespoons milk
Dash of Worcestershire sauce – Dad's taste secret
Sea salt and ground black pepper
115g (4oz) cheese slices

Heat the butter in a 24cm (9½in.) frying pan at medium heat. Add potato and keep stirring to brown lightly. Spread evenly over the pan. Turn on the grill at medium. Beat the eggs, milk, sauce, salt and pepper together. Pour the egg mixture into the pan. Using the flat blade of a palette knife, gently draw egg inwards from the pan edge so that the egg runs through the potato and cooks. While the top is still runny, quickly lift under the grill for a few seconds to set. Top with overlapping slices of cheese. Grill to melt, bubble and brown. Serve from the pan with a simple tomato salad.

Soufflé style

Separate the yolks and whites of two eggs. Beat egg yolks and milk together. Whisk whites stiffly and fold into the egg mix. Cook as above. The cheese puffs as it melts – yummy.

Tattie salad

Pouring dressing over warm tatties adds depth of flavour to a salad.

___

Serves 4
550g (1lb 4oz) potatoes (AR/W/N)
1 tablespoon white wine or cider vinegar
½ teaspoon sea salt
Ground black pepper
1 tablespoon chopped fresh chives or spring onions
1½ teaspoon each of mayonnaise and Greek yoghurt mixed together

___

Boil the potatoes in salted water till tender, drain well. Mix the vinegar, sea salt, ground black pepper and half the chives and pour over the warm potatoes in a bowl and shake gently. Infuse for 1 hour. Gently mix in the rest of the chives and mayonnaise mix. Serve garnished with a few snipped chives.

Tarragon, chervil or parsley may also be added. Store sealed in the fridge for up to 2 days.

Swabian kartoffelsalat

My friend Gisela writes:'According to my family in
Stuttgart this potato salad is the most savoury in
Germany.'

Serves 6
750g (1lb10oz) scrubbed small new potatoes

Dressing:
Pinch of sugar
¼ teaspoon sea salt
A little white pepper
2 tablespoons onion, finely chopped
2½ tablespoons cider vinegar
60ml (2fl oz) vegetable stock

To finish:
5 tablespoons olive oil

Cook the potatoes in boiling salted water till tender.
Drain. Slice into a bowl when cool enough to handle.
Mix the dressing ingredients and pour over warm
potatoes, shake to coat, infuse for 20 minutes, stir in oil
and serve. *Guten appetit!*

Soups

Cullen skink

I learned to make Cullen skink in the kitchens of
Baxter's staff canteen. The secret lies in a 'floury tattie'
which disintegrates to a satisfying gloopiness as the soup
pot simmers. Original recipes use Finnan haddock,
involving removal of fish bones. Smoked fillet makes life
easier for the soup maker.

Serves 4

1 onion, finely chopped
550g (1lb 4oz) potatoes, peeled and chopped (F)
450ml (¾pt) creamy milk
600ml (1pt) water
450g (1lb) undyed smoked haddock fillet
30g (1oz) butter
Sea salt and ground black pepper
150ml (¼pt) double cream (optional)
Chopped fresh parsley or chives to garnish (optional)

Put the onions and potatoes into a deep soup pot, pour in
the milk and water, bring to the boil, reduce the heat,
cover and simmer for 40 to 45 minutes or till the potatoes
are softly disintegrating. Lay the fish on top of the soup,
cover to simmer for 5 minutes till the fish is cooked.
Reduce the heat, flake the fish through the soup, stir in
the butter and season to taste. Serve hot, garnished with
freshly chopped parsley or chives and a swirl of cream.

If not sufficiently thick, stir in some mash.

Potato, celeriac and apple soup

During the 1970s I shared a flat at Innes House, near Elgin, and made friends with other residents over shared meals, wine and chat. We remain in touch. Delicious soup served at our last party inspired my friend Veronica to experiment. The result is stunning.

Serves 4

15ml (1 tablespoon) vegetable oil
225g (8oz) potato, peeled and chopped (F/AR)
350g (12oz) celeriac, peeled and chopped
115g (4oz) eating apple, peeled, cored and chopped
1 stick celery, cleaned and chopped
30g (1oz) root ginger, peeled and chopped
1 litre (1¾pt) vegetable or chicken stock
Lemon juice
Sea salt and ground black pepper
Nutmeg

To serve:
Chopped toasted walnuts
Crumbled stilton cheese

Heat the oil in a deep pan on medium heat, add the vegetables, apple and ginger, and stir to soften. Add the stock, boil, reduce the heat to simmer covered for 45 minutes till tender. Blitz smooth, season to taste, adding a pinch of nutmeg and squeeze of lemon juice to enhance flavour. Serve hot topped with walnuts and/or stilton!

Vichyssoise

Friends invited two couples for dinner on consecutive
weekends, but confusion with dates caused 'double
booking'. Hostess Joy had made vichyssoise sufficient for
the extra diners but was short of one portion for herself.
A professional actress, used to improvising, she passed off
a plate of cold milk topped with chopped grass as one of
the best soups she had ever made. The diners whole-
heartedly agreed, and even asked for the recipe!

Serves 4
15g (½oz) butter
60g (2oz) onion, chopped
60g (2oz) white leek, shredded
60g (2oz) celery, finely chopped
1 litre (1¼pt) vegetable stock
450g (1lb) potatoes, peeled and cubed (F/AR)
Sea salt and ground black pepper
120ml (4fl oz) double cream
Chopped chives

Melt the butter in a deep pan on low heat. Add the
onion, leek and celery. Stir for 2 minutes to soften but
not colour. Add the potato, stir to soften for 2 minutes.
Add the stock, boil and reduce the heat to simmer for 30
minutes. Blitz smooth and season to taste.

Traditionally served cold

Softly whip the cream and fold into the chilled soup. Serve garnished with chopped chives.

Served hot

Stir in double cream and adjust seasoning. Serve hot garnished with chopped chives and/or parsley.

Spicy tomato and tattie soup

The Portsoy Co-op raises funds for charity at a soup and sweet lunch in the hall. The Station Hotel across the road is always pleased to provide soup. Feedback for this one was positive.

Serves 4
2 tablespoons olive oil
1 large onion, peeled and chopped
185g (6oz) carrot, peeled and chopped
85g (3oz) turnip, chopped
450g (1lb) potato, peeled and chopped (F/AR)
2 fresh garlic cloves, peeled and crushed
5cm (2in.) root ginger, peeled and chopped
2 x 250ml (8fl oz) cartons of sieved tomato
600ml (1pt) vegetable stock
Sea salt
Ground black pepper
1 teaspoon smoked paprika

To serve:
Chopped parsley
Double cream

Heat the oil in a deep pan on medium, add the vegetables, potatoes, garlic and ginger and stir to soften for 3 minutes. Add the tomato and stock. Boil, reduce to simmer covered for 45 minutes. Blitz smooth, season with sea salt, ground black pepper and smoked paprika.

Serve hot with a swirl of double cream (if liked) and chopped parsley.

Twenty-minute tattie and leek soup

Invented coming in late from a frosty shopping trip. My lunch guest Jim and I emptied the pan – the sign of a good soup!

Serves 2

85g (3oz) leeks, finely chopped
45g (1½oz) onion, chopped
85g (3oz) carrot, finely grated
175g (6oz) potato, grated (F/AR/W)
2.5cm (1in.) root ginger, peeled and chopped
750ml (1¼pt) stock or water
Sea salt and ground black pepper

Put the vegetables and ginger into a deep pan, add the water or stock and boil. Cover, lower the heat to simmer for 20 minutes. Ladle a third of the soup into a bowl and blitz smooth. Return to the pan, season to taste and re-heat. Serve hot with oatcakes.

Wee dumplings

An optional extra, found in an old book.

Makes 8 hazelnut-size dumplings
50g (1¾oz) mashed potato (F/AR/W)
30g (1oz) oatmeal
1 level teaspoon baking powder
Sea salt and ground black pepper
Broth from soup

Mix the mash, oatmeal and baking powder, and season.
Mix to a stiff dough with broth. Roll into hazelnut-size
balls. Drop into simmering soup, cover, steam for 5
minutes. Serve in the soup.

Main meals

Scots potato pies

A 'no pastry' pie, peculiar to Scotland, with many
regional variations.

Serves 2
2 large potatoes of equal size, peeled thinly (F/AR)
1 tablespoon dripping or oil

Filling:
115g (4oz) minced cooked meat – beef, lamb, venison, chicken
   or game
1 small onion, peeled, chopped, blanched for 5 minutes in
   boiling water and drained
Brown sauce or gravy
Sea salt
Ground black pepper

Turn on the oven at 200°C (fan 180°C), 400°F, Gas 6.
Put the dripping/oil in a deep-sided baking tin into
which the potatoes fit with room to crisp. Cut a 5cm
(1in.) top off each potato. Hollow the centre, leaving a
rim of 1cm (½in.). For stability cut a small slice from the
base of each. Mix the meat and onion, moisten with
brown sauce/gravy, season to taste. Fill each potato and
replace the tops. Heat the baking tin for 2 minutes. Stand
the potatoes upright in the tin and baste with fat. Roast
for 1 hour, basting occasionally. Test with the point of a

skewer after 45 minutes; some potatoes cook more
quickly. Serve hot with gravy.

Other fillings
Minced chicken and ham
Cumberland sausage
Haggis

Banffshire potato pies
For this variation, make a filling with 60g breadcrumbs,
1 egg yolk, chopped herbs, a little milk and melted butter.
Grated cheese or flaked smoked haddock may be added.

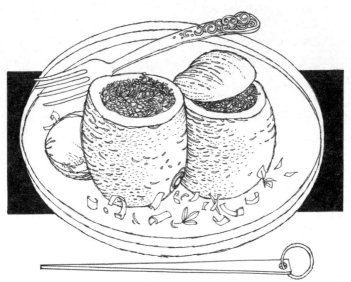

Posh fish pie

This pie travels well. Its prototype survived a drive to Aberdeenshire where lunch guests gave it twelve marks out of ten!

Serves 4 to 6

85g (3oz) fresh salmon fillet
85g (3oz) fresh hake or other firm white fish
Bay leaf
A few peppercorns
Generous squeeze of fresh lemon juice
450ml (15fl oz) milk
115g (4oz) fresh haddock
115g (4oz) smoked haddock fillet
85g (3oz) prawns

Sauce:

30g (1oz) margarine
15g (½oz) butter
45g (1½oz) plain flour
Poaching liquid
Milk if needed
15ml (1 tablespoon) fresh lemon juice
10g (¼oz) grated hard cheese
Sea salt and ground black pepper
Pinch of nutmeg

Topping:
450g (1lb) potatoes, peeled and cut into cubes (F/AR)
15g (½oz) melted butter
225g (8oz) celeriac, peeled and cut into cubes
10g (¼oz) grated hard cheese

––––––––––––––––

Turn on the oven at 180°C (fan 160°C), 350°F, Gas 4.
Butter a wide pie dish 20cm x 25cm (8in. x 10in.). Put
the salmon and hake, bay leaf, peppercorns, lemon juice
and milk into a pan. Boil, lower the heat to simmer for 4
minutes. Add the haddock, simmer for a further 4
minutes. Turn off the heat. Meanwhile cover the potatoes
in cold salted water, boil, lower the heat to simmer till
tender. Cook the celeriac in boiling salted water till
tender. Lift the fish onto a plate, discard the bay leaf and
peppercorns. Reserve the milk. Cut the fish into chunky
pieces, check for bones and set aside. Make a sauce by
melting the margarine and butter together on low, add
flour and stir to a smooth paste. Use a balloon whisk to
beat in the fishy milk to make a pouring sauce. Add more
milk if needed. Stir in the cheese and lemon juice, season
with salt, pepper and nutmeg. Fold in the fish and pour
into the prepared dish. Drain the potatoes, steam dry,
mash with melted butter. Drain the celeriac well, mash
smooth. Beat into the potato then spread over the fish.
Dust with cheese. Bake for 30 minutes till crisp on top.
Serve with salad and plum tomatoes.

Harry's one-pot pheasant

My neighbour Harry likes pheasant; his wife Iris less so.
An oversupply of the bird gave me food, or should I say
'game' for thought! They both enjoyed the result.

Serves 2
300g (10oz) pheasant – leg and thigh, skinned, trimmed
15g (1 tablespoon) cornflour, seasoned with sea salt and
    ground black pepper
60g (2oz) onion, finely chopped
1 eating apple, peeled, cored and chopped
1 small stick celery, finely chopped
350g (12oz) potatoes, peeled and sliced (F/AR/W/N)
Sea salt
Ground black pepper
300ml (½pt) vegetable or chicken stock

Turn on the oven at 150°C (fan 130°C), 300°F, Gas 2.
Toss the pheasant in seasoned cornflour. Put half the
pheasant into the base of a casserole dish, add half the
apple and celery, cover with a thin layer of potato. Season
and repeat. Finish with a thicker layer of sliced potato.
Pour the stock over. Season lightly. Cover, cook slowly
for 1 hour 45 minutes. Turn oven to 180°C (fan 160°C),
350°F, Gas 4. Remove lid to brown the top for 15
minutes. Serve scattered with chopped parsley.

Dounby saus 'n' cheesy tatties

Dounby Primary teacher Nicola Moar created this recipe with her cooking class, using the Dounby butcher's sausages, Orkney butter, milk and cheese, Westray Fairtrade chutney and Birsay tatties grown by school bus driver Ronnie Ballantyne.

Didn't they do well!

_____

Serves 4
8 butcher's sausages, cooked and sliced
600g (1lb 5oz) boiled potatoes, cooled and sliced (F/AR/W/N)
2 dessertspoons chutney

Sauce:
45g (1½oz) butter
45g (1½oz) plain flour
500ml (16fl oz) milk
115g (4oz) mature Orkney cheddar cheese
Sea salt and ground black pepper

Topping:
45g (1½oz) oatmeal
30g (1oz) fresh bread crumbs
115g (4oz) crumbled farmhouse cheese

_____

Turn on the oven at 160°C (fan 140°C), 325°F, Gas 3. Butter a medium-size lasagne dish. Melt the butter, stir in the flour to a smooth paste, and gradually stir in the milk.

Keep stirring till the sauce boils and thickens. Lower the heat, stir in the cheese, season to taste and remove from the cooker. Layer half the sliced potatoes in the base of the dish, pour a quarter of the sauce over and cover with the sliced sausages. Spread with chutney and cover with the rest of the potatoes. Pour over the remaining cheese sauce. Mix the oatmeal and breadcrumbs and sprinkle over along with the crumbled cheese. Bake for 20 to 25 minutes till bubbling and the top is crisp. Serve hot.

Cotter's Saturday night pie

Burns's 'The Cotter's Saturday Night' made me wonder what the frugal wife had in her larder. Neeps, carrots, leeks, tatties, oatmeal in the girnel, milk and butter 'frae the coo!'

But now the supper crowns their simple board …
The dame brings forth, in complimental mood,
To grace the lad, her weel-hain'd kebbuck, fell;
And aft he's prest, and aft he ca's it guid:

Serves 4

Base:
150g (5oz) mince
45g (1½oz) onion, finely chopped
115g (4oz) carrots, peeled and diced
60g (2oz) turnips, peeled and diced
45g (1½oz) leeks, finely chopped
30g (1oz) oatmeal
Water
Sea salt and ground black pepper

Topping:
225g (8oz) grated cooked potato (F/AR/W/N)
45g (1½oz) oatmeal
45g (1½oz) crumbly farmhouse cheese
15g (½oz) butter

Turn on the oven at 180°C (fan 160°C), 350°F, Gas 4. Butter a pie dish 20cm x 25cm (8in. x 10in.). Put the mince in a saucepan, stirring with a wooden spoon to brown and separate the meat grains. Add the onion, stir to brown a little. Mix in the vegetables and oatmeal. Stir in sufficient water to cover, boil, lower the heat, cover and simmer for 45 minutes, stirring occasionally. Add water if needed. Season to taste and pour into the pie dish. Mix the grated potato, cheese and oatmeal and scatter on top and dot with butter. Bake for 25 minutes till browned and bubbling. Serve hot with oatcakes.

May ye 'aft ca' it guid'!

Puddings

Tattie lemon tart

A classic, tangy pudding compared with sweeter lemon meringue pie.

Makes a 20cm (8in.) round tart

Pastry:
115g (4oz) self-raising flour
45g (1½oz) mashed potato (F/AR)
60g (2oz) margarine
15g (½oz) caster sugar

Filling:
2 large eggs
85g (3oz) caster sugar
Zest of 1 lemon
Juice of 1½ lemons
1 teaspoon lemon extract
100ml (3½fl oz) cream
60g (2oz) warm boiled potato, riced or mashed (AR/W)

Turn on the oven at 190°C (fan 170°C), 375°F, Gas 5. Put the pastry ingredients in a mixing bowl and fork into a dough. Turn onto a floured board, knead smooth and roll out to line a 20cm (8in.) diameter tart tin. Prick with a fork, chill for 10 minutes. Bake blind for 12 to 15 minutes, remove the lining and bake for 5 to 10 minutes to dry. Remove from the oven and lower the heat to 150°C (fan 130°C), 300°F, Gas 2. Beat the eggs, sugar, lemon rind, lemon juice and extract together in a bowl. In a separate bowl beat the cream and potato till smooth. Beat the lemon and potato mixes together. Pour into the tart case. Bake for 30 minutes till set. Serve warm or chilled.

If liked, strain lemon mix to remove rind before adding to the potato mix.

Little lemon puds
Pour the filling into buttered ramekins. Bake in a water bath for 20 minutes till set. Serve warm or chilled.

Raspberry tattie bakewell

From a recipe restricted by wartime rationing.

___

Makes a 20cm (8in.) round tart

Pastry:
115g (4oz) self-raising flour
45g (1½oz) mashed or riced potato (F/AR)
60g (2oz) margarine
15g (½oz) caster sugar

Bakewell filling:
60g (2oz) margarine
60g (2oz) caster sugar
60g (2oz) cooked mashed potato
1 egg
1 teaspoon vanilla or almond essence
60g (2oz) self-raising flour sifted with 1 level teaspoon baking powder
1 tablespoon raspberry jam

___

Turn on the oven to heat at 180°C (fan 160°C), 350°F,
Gas 4. Put the pastry ingredients into a bowl, fork into a
dough. Turn onto a floured board, knead smooth and roll
out to line a 20cm (8in.) round tin. Cream the margarine
and sugar till light, beat in the potato, egg and essence,
then fold in the sifted flour and baking powder. Spread
the jam on the pastry base. Cover evenly with sponge
mixture. Bake for 20 to 25 minutes till firm and golden
or the point of a skewer inserted in the middle comes

out clean. Dust with caster sugar. Serve warm with cream or custard as a dessert or serve cool, drizzled with lemon water ice, as a tea cake.

Lemon water ice
Mix sifted icing sugar with fresh lemon juice to a thin smooth paste. Drizzle off a spoon or the prongs of a fork.

Baking and confectionery

Baking

TATTIE OATCAKES · SPELT ·LEFSE·
CRISPBREADS·
·POTATO APPLE AND CINNAMON
LOAF CAKE · FRUITY TATTIE BUNS
·MISREAD MACAROON BAR ·
·CHOCOLATE TATTIE TRUFFLES·
·MASHED TATTIE GLUTEN FREE
DROPPED SCONES
·CHOCOLATE POTATO FUDGE BROWNIE ·

Confectioner

Potato oatcakes for cheese

For those who find oatcake making a challenge, add potato. A dream to knead, roll and cut, baking to an even crisp. Delicious warm from the oven with or without cheese!

___

Makes 60 x 5cm round biscuits
225g (8oz) fine or medium oatmeal
60g (2oz) mashed or riced potato (F/AR)
3g (½ teaspoon) sea salt
1g (scant ¼ teaspoon) bicarbonate of soda
26ml (scant 2 tablespoons) vegetable oil
Water to mix
Oatmeal or rice flour to roll out

___

Turn on the oven at 180°C (fan 160°C), 350°F, Gas 4. Use a food mixer. Put the oatmeal, potato, salt, bicarbonate of soda and oil into the mixing bowl. Mix on slow speed, gradually adding tepid water in stages, until a smooth pliable clean dough is formed. The sound of the mixer will change as the dough comes together. Turn out the dough and dust with oatmeal or rice flour. Knead smooth. Roll out thinly and cut into 5cm (2in.) round biscuits. Put onto a non-stick baking tray. Alternatively divide the dough into four pieces, roll each into a thin round and cut across the diameter to make 4,

6 or 8 triangles depending on desired size. (Scots refer to the triangles as farls and the round of dough a bannock.) Bake for 12 to 15 minutes till crisp and cool on a wire rack. Store sealed in an airtight container.

Add flavour
1 teaspoon rough black pepper
5g (1 teaspoon) grated hard cheese
1 teaspoon dried mixed herbs or 1 tablespoon of fresh

Tattie and spelt crispbreads

A rustic flatbread with taste and crunch to the last bite.

Makes 18 fingers

100g (3½oz) boiled potatoes, riced or mashed (F/AR)
60g (2oz) spelt flour sifted with
1 teaspoon baking powder
2.5g (½ teaspoon) sea salt
10ml (2 teaspoons) oil
Spelt flour to roll

Heat the oven to 180°C (fan 160°C), 350°F, Gas 4. Put the mashed potatoes in a bowl, sift in the flour and baking powder. Add the salt and oil. Fork mix into a pliable dough. Knead smooth on a floured board then cut in two. Roll each thinly to a rectangle 10cm (4in.) wide and prick well. Cut across each rectangle in 5cm (2in.) slices and lay on a non-stick baking tray. Bake for 15 to 20 minutes till crisp. Check after 10 minutes; if colouring quickly reduce oven temperature to 170°C (fan 140°C), 325°F, Gas 4, to ensure a crisp result. Cool on a wire tray and store in an airtight tin.

Blitzed sunflower or pumpkin seeds add crunch, nutrition and taste.

Potato, apple and cinnamon loaf cake

A winner for coffee mornings and fundraising teas.
Moistly more-ish to the last crumb.

Makes 2 x 350g (12oz) loaf cakes
45g (1½oz) honey
85g (3oz) soft brown sugar
115g (4oz) margarine
85g (3oz) raw potato, grated (F/AR)
115g (4oz) apple, grated
225g (8oz) self-raising flour
3 teaspoons cinnamon
1 teaspoon baking powder
2 eggs, beaten

Turn on the oven at 180°C (fan 160°C), 350°F, Gas 4,
and line two loaf tins. Warm the honey, brown sugar and
margarine in a pan. Put the grated potato and apple in a
bowl. Sift in the flour, cinnamon and baking powder.
Mix together. Pour in the pan contents and mix to a soft
dropping consistency with the beaten egg. Divide evenly
between the loaf tins and bake for 20 to 25 minutes till
firm and the point of a skewer inserted in the middle
comes out clean. Cool in the tins, wrap in foil and store
in an airtight container. Keep for up to a week in a cool
place. Freeze for up to two months.

Fruity tattie buns

During the war ingredients were scarce. Adding mashed potato to baking stretched meagre rations.

Makes 8 muffin cakes
30g (1oz) margarine
30g (1oz) caster sugar
115g (4oz) plain mashed potato (F/AR)
30g (1oz) chunky marmalade or apricot jam
2 teaspoons baking powder
85g (3oz) self-raising flour
1 egg beaten with milk to mix
30g (1oz) chopped dried apricot
Caster or icing sugar to finish

Turn on the oven at 180°C (fan 160°C), 350°F, Gas 4. Line eight muffin tins with paper cases. Cream the margarine and sugar till pale, beat in the mashed potato and marmalade or jam. Sift in the flour and baking powder. Mix to a soft dropping consistency with the egg and milk. Fold in the dried apricot and divide evenly between the muffin cases. Bake for 12 to 15 minutes till risen and firm and the point of a skewer inserted in the middle comes out clean. Cool on a wire rack. Dust with icing or caster sugar and enjoy freshly baked.

Lefse (Norwegian potato pancakes)

My Norwegian friend Espen's favourite soft flatbread, which he enjoys warm rolled with butter, cinnamon and sugar. Some fill lefse with jam, berries or peanut butter! What will you enjoy in yours?

Makes 12 small lefse (pancakes)

Step 1
225g (8oz) mashed potato (F/AR)
15g (½oz) melted butter
½ teaspoon salt
15ml (1 tablespoon) double cream
Mix together. Keep in the fridge overnight.

Step 2
115g (4oz) self-raising flour
Flour to dust
Brown rice flour (optional)

Put the potato mix in a bowl. Break into fine crumbs with a fork, then work in the flour, finally kneading to form a smooth slightly sticky dough. Flour work surface well (I find rice flour less sticky). Turn out the dough, divide into 12 equal pieces, rolling each into a ball. Roll each ball into a thin circle. Heat a thick-bottomed frying pan on medium. The heat is correct when a bead of water dropped on the surface sizzles and evaporates. Bake one pancake at a time. Roll the next while the previous one is cooking. In less than a minute the underside will be browning, turn, bake, then fold in a clean tea towel on a plate to keep warm. Repeat. (I found it difficult to start but soon got into the rhythm.) Serve warm, freshly baked. Store in a sealed bag or box in the fridge for up to a week. Interleaf with baking parchment, seal in a bag or container and freeze for up to six weeks.

Re-heat lefse by running a clean wet hand over the surface to dampen. Heat in a warm frying pan, oven or under the grill. Norwegian lefse bakers use a grooved rolling pin.

Canadian potato candy

Orcadian Margaret Rendall gave me this recipe from
Canada, where she lived for many years.

Makes 40 walnut-size candies
60g (2oz) plain mashed potato (F/AR)
15g (½oz) butter
1 teaspoon vanilla or almond essence
225g (8oz) icing sugar – approximately

Finish with:
Walnut or almond halves
Chocolate vermicelli
Cocoa powder
Melted dark chocolate

Mix the mashed potato and butter and beat in the
essence and sifted icing sugar. The mixture will be fluid
but stiffens to a fondant consistency. Wear food gloves to
knead smooth. Roll teaspoon-size pieces into balls. Lay
on a plate. Sandwich between two nut halves, roll in
cocoa powder or chocolate vermicelli.

To dip in melted chocolate, chill to firm. Use a
cocktail stick to dip in chocolate. Before the chocolate
sets, coat with chopped nuts or coconut. Set on a tray
lined with non-stick paper. Keep in the fridge for up to a
week. Arrange a selection in fancy cellophane bags or
boxes as a gift.

Misread macaroon bar

Scottish Women's Institute enthusiast Iris McIntosh
found a recipe for potato macaroons which I misread.
This is the outcome.

Makes 1 slab approximately 20cm x 25cm (8in. x 10in.)
115g (4oz) desiccated coconut, toasted under a medium grill
100g (3½oz) mashed potato (F/AR)
1 teaspoon vanilla essence
1 knob of butter
450g (1lb) icing sugar
150g (3½oz) dark cooking chocolate

Put the potato into a bowl and beat in the icing sugar
to make a stiff fondant-like paste. Stir in the coconut.
Roll out the paste to approximately 20cm x 25cm
(8in. x 10in.), lay into a non-stick tray. Set in a cool place.
Melt chocolate, spread over the slab, set, then cut into
fingers. Do not chill in the fridge. The chocolate
becomes brittle and breaks off the coconut interior.

Keeps for up to a week in the fridge.

Chocolate tattie truffles

My first attempt would have cured any chocoholic. I persevered!

Makes 14

75g (2½oz) cold mashed potato (F/AR)
5g (1 teaspoon) melted butter
½ teaspoon vanilla essence
15ml (1 tablespoon) runny honey, maple or agave syrup
5g (1 teaspoon) icing sugar
15g (½oz) cocoa powder

To coat:
Finely chopped hazelnuts, walnuts or pistachios
Shredded coconut
Cocoa powder
or
150g (3½oz) dark or milk chocolate

Put the truffle ingredients in a bowl and fork to a stiff smooth paste. Wear food gloves for the next step. Put topping ingredients on separate flat plates. Roll teaspoons of mix into balls, then in toppings to coat. Lay on a flat plate. Set in the fridge. Keep chilled in a sealed container for up to 5 days.

To coat truffles in chocolate, freeze for 10 to 15 minutes. Cover a flat plate with non-stick baking paper.

Using a double boiler or microwave, 75 per cent melt the chocolate, remove from the heat and beat to a coating consistency. Spear each truffle with a cocktail stick, dip into the chocolate then lay on the non-stick paper. Chill to set. Leftover chocolate if not overheated may be stored and reused.

Flavours to try
Dark chocolate ginger – 15g (½oz) chopped crystallised
    ginger
Mocha – 2 teaspoons strong coffee
Chocolate orange – 1 teaspoon grated orange rind and 1
    teaspoon orange oil
Free from – omit butter, bind with extra honey or syrup

Gluten-free

Chocolate potato fudge brownie

Mash imparts unique sumptuousness – 'the brownie eating experience'! Creating a 'can't tell it's gluten-free' cake is difficult. I think this one fits the bill, or should I say plate!

Makes a cake 18 x 30cm (7 x 12in)
100ml (3½oz) sunflower oil
85g (3oz) soft brown sugar
85g (3oz) boiled, mashed or riced potato (F/AR)
2 large eggs, beaten
115g (4oz) dark chocolate
150g (5oz) gluten-free self-raising flour
1 teaspoon vanilla essence
30g (1oz) chopped walnuts

Turn on the oven at 180°C (fan 160°C) 350°F, Gas 4. Oil and line a non-stick baking tin. Beat the eggs, oil, sugar and potatoes together. Melt the chocolate on medium power in the microwave or in a bowl over simmering water, stirring till the chocolate is smooth. Beat one tablespoon of the potato mix into the chocolate. Pour the chocolate into the potato mix, sift in the flour, add the vanilla essence and beat till smooth. Stir in the walnuts. Pour into the baking tin, spread evenly. Bake for 15 minutes or till the cake is firm and springy and the point of a skewer comes out clean. Cool in the tin. Spread with topping when cold. Chill for 10 minutes to set. Cut and enjoy. Store wrapped in foil in a cool place.

Chocolate potato fudge topping

6og (2oz) butter, melted
30g (1oz) cocoa powder
45g (1½oz) boiled mashed or riced potato (F/AR)
30g (1oz) golden syrup
1 teaspoon instant coffee powder
60g (2oz) icing sugar

Beat the ingredients to a thick spreading consistency. Add more icing sugar to thicken if needed.

Mashed tattie gluten-free dropped scones

An afternoon tea party was an opportunity to experiment, normal versus gluten-free with added mash. Guests voted for the mash! The scones remained moist the following day.

Makes 6 to 8 dropped scones
115g (4oz) gluten-free self-raising flour
60g (2oz) plain boiled mashed potato
1 teaspoon gluten-free baking powder
1 egg, beaten
30g (1oz) golden syrup or honey
100ml (3fl oz) milk or dairy-free coconut milk

Heat a girdle or thick-bottomed frying pan on medium heat. Sift the flour and baking powder into a bowl. Add the potato, egg and syrup or honey. Mix with the milk to a thick smooth batter. Use a balloon whisk for lump-free lightness. Test the heat of the girdle with a dust of flour. The temperature is right if it turns golden; reduce the heat if it burns. Rub with oil. Bake tablespoons of batter till bubbles rise and burst. Flip over with a palette knife or fish slice. Tap gently to release trapped air to ensure an even bake. Cool on a wire rack wrapped in a clean tea towel and eat fresh. Indulgence is to drop dark chocolate chips onto the soft uncooked scone surface as it bubbles, flip over to melt and bake. A messy eat but worth it!

Mabel Thomson's tattie wine

Richard Shearer remembers earlier years when a glass or two of Mabel Thomson's potent tattie wine was a great lubricant at parties. I asked for the recipe and tasting notes. Richard was happy to oblige. 'Here is the Tattie Wine recipe (hic!) as promised.'

---

6 medium-size old tatties, washed, peeled and sliced (F/AR/W)
2 lemons and 2 oranges, washed, peeled and sliced
1.3kg (3lb) sugar
450g (1lb) raisins
4.55 litres (1 gallon) water
30g (1oz) brewer's yeast

Place the sliced tatties, lemon and orange in a pot with the raisins and sugar. Pour over boiling water and stir until the sugar is dissolved. When cool but not cold add the yeast. Cover with a tea towel and keep at room temperature. Stir daily for 10 days. Strain and pour into clean sterilised bottles with a tight cap. Leave to cool and store in a cool dark place for 6 to 12 months.

'I will taste in the next few days.'

'What I say is that, if a man really likes potatoes, he must be a pretty decent sort of fellow.'

A.A. Milne